ENGLAND'S EDGING

Part One

2020

Publishing without …

Copthorne

RH10 3RD

Today we'd hole up   but then the seasaw
seasons dragged us stairwards to a bed-spread
world of eiderdowns   Within the night-chilled
house our beds would mass   like fallen graves   We'd
scuttle off   while tongs and poker nuzzled
down   and coals lost their cool through the fireguard
feeding like beasts that rasped with sparks   or dream
beyond dread of being buried and nailed
to our sheets   by those curtains' lid of cold
Each dawn the frosted shrouds were etched in glass.

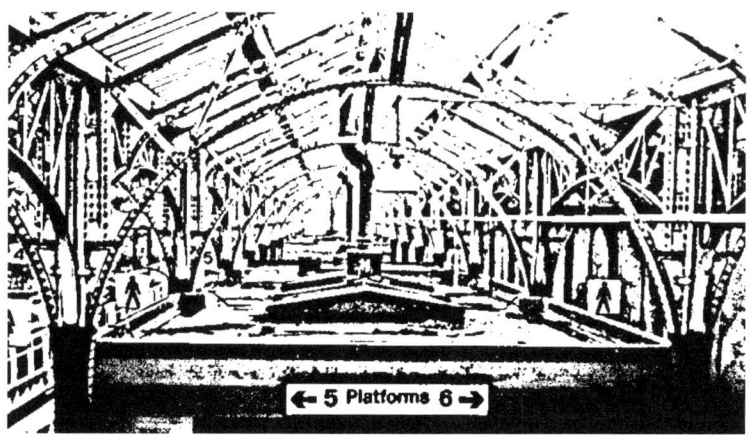

Dover Marine Station

CT17 9DQ

They were wild Western Docks where British rail
ways quit the buffers   and fleets of rucksacks
queued up the peeling platforms   We'd wonder
why the virgin tourists couldn't fathom
how the wrought-iron wreck   was racked by breakers
at England's end   where anglers lost their lines
while everyone else dashed to excavate
beneath clay and chalk   One late day I rolled
in from Belgium   dashed my duty free down
some railings and felt   the break up coming.

A British School In Flanders

TV30 80BE

Six or seven make-do fielders   trip up
a matting wicket   Somewhere an ex-pat
long off teacher stammers an unheard cursed
reminder   *For God's sake, straighten up!*   Who
knows who missed the most   or was more askew
through midweek doldrum dusks   that nudged between
an outfield   rolled out like an English square
To run up there now would spin no surprise
names or quips   Who won   or does that Belgian
museum loom like bones of empire still?

Fugloy

767 HTK

The lost not least village peers at fleeting
harbour calms and ignores the horseshoe sound
which Faroe's choked with limbs of pilot whales
impaled through brine   and dyed by long last wounds
We leap from the mail boat   two Swedes a French
and German pair and several Danes   I pierce
the damp and leave the tufts of random roofs
and hay   The peak shows the clouds that snuff out
this rock   and an English spectre who knows
my road   leans on another harbour's quay.

Caversham

RG4 5BA

More leftover than Latin quarter here
a year homed in   The house faced cars half-cock
snubbed by sashed and baying neighbours   Trees had
quit the avenue which blamed   some builders
council vans   and hated us meanwhile   We
bluffed a lease   and slipped the leash   Phil pilfered
the disaster bedroom almost gassing
us from his coin-fed grate   Then Richard cut
a curse through the tousled lawn   and I dossed
down in a mantrap we'd mustered from bricks.

Spurn Head

HU12 0UG

Yorkshire's new island   Landing here we met
the spit like a hand across the Humber
before the limb got lopped   Drawn by Larkin's
map of words we dodged   those lowering wind-
filled spires   found the callipered track to Spurn
and its freight   spilt like luggage through the dunes
a crane   a slipway   half a lighthouse ringed
the concrete-cradled cottages   each left
or shed after storms   You'd taken off when
it all peeled back through thirty years' thin air.

George Street South

SP2 7BQ

We got off slightly   Our road was a scar
on the city's torso   twenty-five years
after Meadow and George Street were undone
by diggers   two lags left limp for dotage
Hardly Berlin   but the hacking asphalt
bustled and flickered through our first three years
Churchill's Way perhaps   Before the last drive
one wayward trip wheeled us to the tourist
side   and our terrace's score of cousins
each numbered with the ousted souls of homes.

Bemerton Heath

SP2 9HS

Salisbury's brink was an isolation ward
before the poisonings   Out to the west
homes wore well towards the downland   and play-
grounds trussed their wooded knot   The heath hill ailed
and its tourniquet bus loops bound each street
to the inclines   as if they were woundings
The school's rebranded like some loud shirt   Once
I glared across a score of wooden desks
to the cuff   Threadbare stubble wove its weft
and a doe   steered fawns   warping down   barbed wire.

Alexandra Park

WA10 3TP

The best place for meetings   a crux or crutch
from fifty years ago when the workers
knew how this could work   Fleeing work to meet
there takes me past the grand condemned canteen
then the bay-blue turret chequered by Pilk.'s
and its cell   draped with a hawk's eye billboard
of lives at work that worked out here   The seams
have sealed   Glass furnaces were reek by jowl
with sidings   a new school   saplings   and lakes
and houses queuing up   where families worked.

Dunkirk

NG7 2JY

I sneaked you in to the city's blister
disguised by Sundays   wrested from the loops
and queues of Nottingham   There's one opening
to Lace Street   cushioned by a ghost office
corner that snookers these emptied streets   urged
on by trains   and a splash of canal   Yours
was an up-against-everything terrace
a warren of wanderers   fathoming
how to grow up or grasp Englishness   purged
by the fumes and the din that drenched their homes.

Montgomery

SY15 6PA

Those grey spare hours and bracing B-roads   one
false mood and here I lodge   brought short and soaked
by no-man's-lands   What's happened to the warmth
of Shropshire   carried off as June became
a condensation vanishing?   I drive
past England   take a right   and cross the worn
down Dyke of a hidden border   Over
its roofs the town breathes out the sighs of Wales
while the Long Mind sulks   From the trig point shafts
of clouded pine have nowhere in their sights

Bishop's Castle

SY9 5AE

Shropshire's back   Less than an hour on last-leg
roads and I park where the market clangs   bare
and a high street away from that stunted
church   There's a climb   to water colour out
posts   and shop front souvenirs   next to hand-
me-down booths   tea slops   and banks on the brink
But the bishop's   quit this parish   leaving
unremembered castles over the town
and the enemy's moss   or buckled kerbs
ivy winters   where dog talk fills short cuts.

West Bexington

DT2 9DF

Booking this house had spooked me with its crass
happenstance   Coleman and Tennant parked once
by the drive to solve who'd done what or how
dissecting this drain-straight dead-end incline
into slices of fiction   Up Beach Road
I pause   and imagine summer   Dorset's
of infinite shingle   and hand-stitched fields
But we're trapped by those half-fledged gulls   over-
night anglers   and uncleared paths to National
Trust barricades   Whatever next?   *Keep Out.*

Dorchester

DT1 2FN

We began at his end by that bedless
room where Hardy's heart was carved out to store
with the biscuits overnight   The kitchen
hid   near that overhung window where Tess
was hatched-snatched-and-dragged through the cold-charted
pastures of Wessex   Somehow half the heart
was scoffed by a desperate feline   Cat
pure woman   and writer were ruptured fall-
ing   Remember the flag when it ended
as you looked across to Winchester gaol?

Malvern Link

WR14 2HX

Linking more hooves here would set up the last
run to Malvern   Look to the gradient
hauling you high beyond B-and-B's   blue
plaques and furtive paths   stealing a nose down
veranda dusks   lichen lanes   and holly-
hocked whitewash   Beyond the forge-red midland
brick   this backyard and yardstick of England
this be-all beginning-all happily
common place   rests under laurels and looks
like it's waiting for a coach and horses ...

Woburn

MK45 2HZ

The sound file's on an older phone   That shriek
before the morning   wove through the wheat-wind
after the Scotch pine margin   Something loud
had rasped beyond the burbles   cracking first
thing   as the serried families woke throughout
their tongue-in-groove encampment   By the wire
I stretched   and peered towards the wilds of sun-
dried pasture tracks and hedgerow   No one came
or wandered past that dingy creek the lake
had over-filled   No voice called   *What the hell ..?*

Wotton-under-Edge

GL12 7BT

It's like an English precipice   almost
too long across somewhere's veldt or prairie
shrunk to nought and then   you parachute down
a switch-backed 1-in-4   miss the escape
lane   kick the brakes   and collide with this limb
of England   Sovereign and suffering no
one's rule   Here are its calling cards   common
and garden chapels that snub the dug up
roads   or overworked coughing shops   edging
out edgy yards   Not special   specially here.

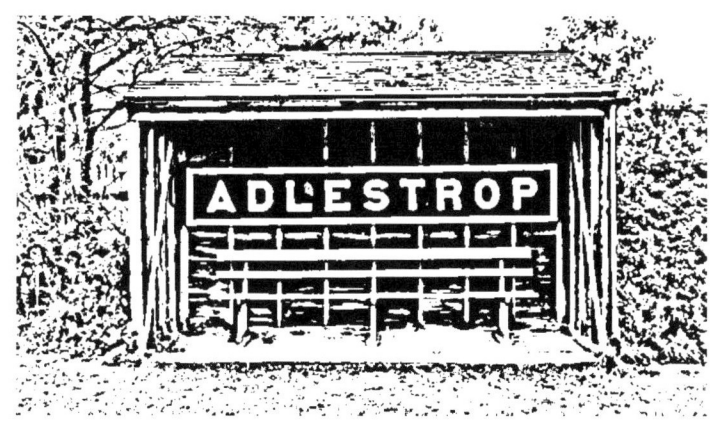

Adlestrop

GL56 0YN

Don't draw up here   Why would you anyway?
I remember regret and   drizzling through
cloud   with Gloucestershire's drying hay   somewhere
beyond my skewed and feeble memory.
It wasn't the absences   No platform
no shaft recoiled from the trenches of time
and least of all   the wrong birds filled the trees
like some encroaching arc lights   fixed to spray
the canopy of cloud   Catch a bus here
and hide with his poem   Look wistful   Leave.

Furtho

MK19 6NR

Head for the new town   but brake where that strip
of Northants   hands over to Milton Keynes
where there'll be bartering over Union
locks   or where Ouse-fields and Watling Street mix
with a slick of A5   The hamlet splits
through the unknotted endings of footpaths
and sheepish hedges   its farm becoming
invisible   There's the unrazed manor
a shell of dry dovecote   and then St. Bart.'s
above the jetty   looking for doubters.

Blakeney

NR25 7BE

Now here the sea's about up to my waist
and it's half a mile to land   See the Point
and all its meadowed silt   is moving west
a longshore drift they call it   Anyways
watch your feet when we moor up   There's a bit
of a gap on the ebb and keep your mutts'
leads on if you're anywhere near the seals
Summerhouse?   No   that's one of those larch lapped
shacks that's kept locked   It's like that here   Try
the lifeboat place   They'll maybe chat you up.

Northwick Park

HA1 3UJ

I was back in the east of 82
dead roads by pale walls and dustsheet drapes   dawn
surrounds Warsaw   We parked by doors that swung
your Boxing Day shift into life   as near
or dear patients stayed low at home   Sometimes
we dither at Watford   minutes away
from that life-long boundary road   where lives
were coloured in by you   Mine slows and greys
time sticks   and I guess how many have signed
off or clocked in since   down those endless wards.

M6 J27

WN5 8TG

Another escape lane where escapades
end with a spine-twitching swerve   towards switch-
backed remaindered turf   It unwinds us like
clockwork cars   launching a life's worth of bursts
into who-went-where   We've edged north   passed firs
trimming the wind fields   and unlocking hay
slopes   and deep leas in Bowland   the grey tops
of Yorkshire   large Lakes   or blind and slow pacts
with the southern mesh   Always that red light
holds up the sliproad   asks do *you* live here?

Middle Eye

CH48 0QG

Penultimate places   like that briny
ungrazed pasture between everywhere   Wales
to the south-west practises mountains   while
Ellesmere parts   from a feather of choking
industrious cloud   and Kirby's gone west
of its alter hedgerows   Here the footpath
wanders up these tidelined broad brush ochre
jowls   The sandstone slumps beneath a plateaued
shock of heather   marooning its soundtrack
soon   like lark-tides   lost in unheard grasses.

Orrell Park

L9 8BU

Aintree's a cut out frame   platforms as plain
as the racecourse is tall and sharp   shaded
in black by Merseyrail's mustard   Stencils
of upland   and some buddleiaed branch line
venture a boundary   but one stop on   trains
pause by hedgerows of hebe and silver
dust verges   under the plastic-cracked arch
of nevergreen baskets   where hanging tubs
bung with pansies   Mares' tails and hyacinth
daff-trials and frayed ferns   copy the feral.

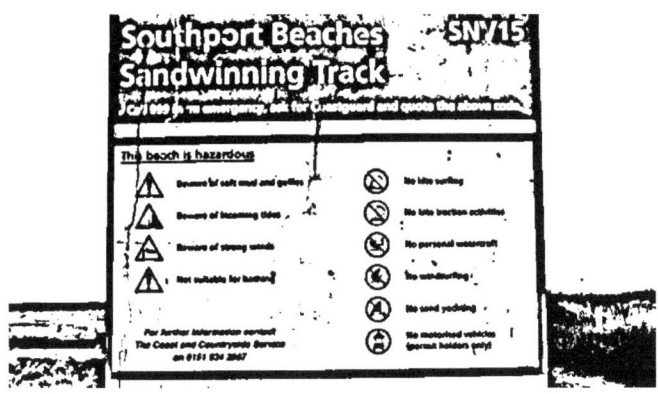

The Sandwinning Track

PR9 9PJ

That walk to the waves   Have you found or dreamt
how it ends   or staggered through grit and sand
to the nowhere marsh?   Imagine a sea
adrift   dawn in August   Clichés amass
and minutes pass   You look at troughs laid out
with cord grass   and cockles   or samphire   spread
like sheets   on thirsty mudflats   Their salt pans
empty   Below the skyline tankers check
that rigs and buoys have cauterized the clouds
Blackpool lurks   There's an aspirin of moon.

LJLA

L24 1YD

If this was the final airport   which flights
would we drag from old holiday holdalls
reviewing our angsty albums?   Cologne
maybe through squalls   or the wrinkled Massif
Friesland staked out by sand-islands   a barbed
Segrada   or the Polish lad vouching
for beers   that Mexican trying to move
his children to Cheshire from Spain?   First off
we booked back seats   like on that Dublin trip
with the girl who'd lost her leg months before.

The Deaf Institute

M1 7HE

For The Delines

A woody bistro   and an ale or three
later   we wound up some black stair-chimney
Beyond a wall of chords penned a sound booth
downlit by blinded glass   like night all day
where you came to light by parroting wall-
paper and unplugged State-side truths   Amy's
words echoed with who we were   how we've been
every which side of the widened ocean
hearing you first in that ear-shifting place
like soundtracks   for our country's hushed up soul.

Bury

BL9 0BW

For Willy Vlautin

Four of us slid past March store sales and plate
glass lies bought pints of fear and remembered
him lost at home We knocked that Sunday back
from sleazy chairs then crossed the soaking street
and met you where that plastered ceiling rose
They'd packed off the seats and you took the hall
by warmth played a set of loss and comfort
and left its list by a foldback You paused
at the death then stepped through a secret door
to sign the songs an evening played for him.

Sunderland Point

LA3 3LL

We finish off   unmarooned   by kindly
tides and watch the cloak of the Lune arise
from the causeway's nape   Then we talk of life
in that esplanade of halfway homes while
no one hoves in from the bluff   or wanders
down the strand   or leaves a guest house terrace
but waders encroach on the stones   like drift
wood   by archives of keels   On another
shore bullocks are salting themselves in swamps
that wrap around Heysham's concrete castle.

AJ Bell Stadium

M30 7LJ

… to the middle of somewhere half-erased
so the ground could arise from the dashes
to Trafford's epic centre   in union
or half a league   We miss the toss   and swim
through the sharks and showers   while drenched cadets
unfurling stuff make brave and brief parades
beside tiny locks and props   The ale runs
dry a minute in   and sixty odd boots
wallow   their studs a penalty quagmire
while rain and the wailing   serve us a draw.

Arnside Knott

LA5 0BL

Colours are leaving early as July
dries   draining the greens that clothe its usual
flux of maybe-cloud breaks from days away
and family-fed cook ups of duty-cum-
guilt served out on greasy lawns   The Knott's not
far   above Arnside's covert homes   that queue
to hear   the rattled rack of trains   salt marsh
lambs   and folk forgetting their memories
Up there I saw it all   the sanded shades
of river-slouch   the bay a sheet of stains.

Penrith Platform 2

CA11 7JQ

The last train strives for Scotland in the stray
light of a lost blank holiday   Somehow
you've legged and burrowed it through Euston's
shut-throat cattle yard   branded luckily
and north enough to break the glut   Penrith
gathers   taxis creeping up by guarded
hatchbacks and outsized minis   directing
reptile-lights at the gothic ticket hall
Our tiny screens light up your train's demise
and boozers rolling north   loom large and loud.

Slaley

NE470AA

I find the last words of a piece   bogged down
by slopes that spread like counties   or drooping
boughs of elms   marooned by a tide of sheep
where the hares jump ship   The lines last as far
as the stub of a church where I return
to join its coffee mob   Ten God-cheerers
pour out scones and tea in winnowing tints
of border talk while   stranger   I write off
that farewell to our country's verge   How many
more Mays will warm these altered table cloths?

Kielder

NE48 1ER

We kept finding beyond behind beyond
from uncounting the signs to the Water
to watching the borderline folds and slopes
of livestocked hides and fleeces   and tracking
the Tyne   We felt reservoirs either side
that filled our windscreen   while miles of fir-trails
buried the peat creeks   Under the currents
railway streaks   farm shapes   school yards   and scuffed lanes
were dead to this end of the wild   We stopped
at the Castle   the blank trunks trudging on.

Walsingham

NR22 6AL

Isn't this wrong and the vestigial proof
of what no one believes in days like these?
What's faith anyhow   Scuttling to Norfolk
and hiding in centuries of hedge-parades
Telling your pals you've retreated to where
the dead ways hold sway?   All those old sliding
doors   fuzzed panes   and random chants   or queuing
to say we've seen the tableau?   There's the hub
properly staged in the village   *Please Don't
Touch*   Miles out the Catholics make do and bend.

Westminster Cathedral

SW1P 1QW

Underneath railway fretworks they're selling
off London's locked up viaducts   Massing
by Victoria one of these junctions
is held up by its pursed strings   The vaulted
cave has rescued the faith from collisions
of Englishness   A crossing which passports
disciples of difference   it shimmers
with hope and mosaics   while beggars wait
stopped at the door   Above   Heaven's brickwork
is black   Is that all we've got when it ends?

Bourton-on-the-Water

GL54 2ER

Two sides to the Windrush   clearly   this one
for penguins   that malibou stork   and rat
runs from Bicester   Another is pushed out
beyond the estates and laid up coach parks
the shack of a Roman hideout   hidden
where industry fits and stalls   It's nowhere
compared to the CofE citadel
armoured   by arms' lengths of oak statement pews
or victorious sponge   We cross a few
bridges   to find the model village sold.

Nether Padley

S32 2JA

April's the more frugal month here   breathing
splinters of spring   up the dust-root walkways
and birch and beech dead ends   as if Easter's
remembered   There are chapels where rain probes
like tubers through their rubbish   in their bones
One's retained its name and a strained glass frieze
above its penthouse keypads   In Bakewell
another lost its holy ghosts last March
The doll's house nave in Tideswell posts more deaths
than Masses   on its cracked unnoticed board.

Kintbury

RG17 9SP

The small sign on a wall   then the llamas
past the gatehouse   and up a rise and wait
before that foot-fallow sweep of under
downland   Berkshire's housed this grave unguarded
face   its door as thick as a rafter   walls
a varnished mirror of hope   conversion
and hidden lives   that wondered and wound up
in faith or fear   Now vocations run quiet
the cedars creak   and windows rust in wings
chucked up in the sixties   and retreating.

Torremolinos

T26 62E

Forgive or take forty years   The landmarks
have moved up that concrete strand   and these new
palms and parasols throw little shade   My
photo shows hotels that smothered the last
powdered farms   but at twelve I encountered
Guardia up every *calle* and Franco's
army of flats down unmade paths   Many
had smelt the slaughter   four decades before
They hid behind shutters   like dry silent
hills   and watched English lads working out Spain.

Fourwentways

CB21 6AP

This ox-bow bend's had twenty years to hide
the secrets of its wandergrowth   and now
the underlay of sedge and sphagnum makes
a soggy low-way   past the fast new flow
of EU-bound   diesel   flooding downstream

You breach the paling   break back through thickets
thickened by card-floored cups or auto-trash
and lose more bearings   But where's the baited
traffic across those forecourts   or dodgy
road-pikes bent on exit   As close as that?

Wallace Monument

FK9 5LF

It's the wrong way   beyond the other plug
across the glacial groove   that left the Forth
to slither through the grazing plain   washing
off or buffing up the remembered wounds
that coerced this kingdom   William's short-
lived statue is long gone   a knave-hearted
jibe at the past   His turret holds the fort
for all that the English need to make out
below   and from the Crown   Every sandstone
step   could stand for another betrayal.

Gretna Services

DG16 5GG

Unless you need to forge a wedding   leave
and fast   the land of dead speed traps and dry
trip times   and cruise the Celtic skies   The route
becomes a helpful high road if   *your eyes*
are fit for driving   when you   *don't drive tired*
Drive smart save fuel   and   *to road conditions*
Remember how   *lifting litter risks road*
workers lives   so *reduce the risk*   Welcome
to Alba   and its habit of speaking
differently   past English indifference.

The Land Settlement, Abington

CB21 6AS

For Epic45

How summer breaks through cornfields   and phantom
clouds like these   where quiet houses lock in
and look out for those who died to sell up
Durham emigres trading coal for clay
The settlement settles to somewhere where
ponies   and 4x4s   mire the holdings
and grassed houses stake out their other rooms
Aga-ed   expanded   hot-tubbed   and alarmed
But some remember the futures they ploughed
the echoes of harvest where lanes don't change.

Bourn Bridge

CB21 6AN

The science park's partitioned   and cameras
nose over fields they've barred   Here's rugby
country   and there are some chirpy Baltic
women bent over veg.   organically
Permissive paths have occupied the wood
and the World Famous Cafe puts up a bund
of cemented wire   across the gap once
called a Welcome   while the listed half-baked
shack next door   is swallowed by a bury-
built school for kids who pay   to learn by trees.

Newman House, Dublin

D02 CC99

The bullets' trace runs up the Fusilier's
Arch and marshals us towards the wounded
ponds   where ducks were shot   Further round the Green
I waffle something to that bench-bound lad
who asks after Brexit   and affably
Later our Northside guide finds who the Brits
laid low in flak streets by the GPO
and at St. Stephen's   builders bar the rooms
where Hopkins taught   and wrote away his ghosts
suffering the ache of his Englishness.

Brixton

SW9 8BN

Patti's riff on writing   whiffs of Left Bank
stark espresso fumes   that blister futures
spike the memory   and muster thoughts of how
once we'd thought we'd always wake like this   But
we walk behind St. James's Park   and meet
London's calm and frozen walls like Paris
with no soul   then Brixton wipes the static
neat disorder once for all   and the up-
ended city scrawls what we'd hoped to see
colouring in   its raw and soiled entrails.

Annandale Water

DG11 IHD

Swallows or cormorants?   The Scottish scores
for the EU poll were called as we breached
the Borders   Cumulus or shallow silt?
Late May's blues on the loch showed the wonder
of what's up there   Fir frieze or fag-ending
bored walk?   That updrafted couple will hunt
the sun in clutches   Dog-drawn or carton-
crouched?   Feathered hulls plummet like underhand
Tridents   Pit stop or sitting to tick off
the looping hills?   Swallows and cormorants.

Vincent Square

SW1P 2PW

Face inward boys so no-one sees us   Hide
the art of distance   You two slide the sight
screens past the lampposts   Block out those joggers
Let's have a squad pretending to bowl fast
at the fleet of nets   Look like you're poking
the wicket   Pad or man up   Take your guard
while the gates swing wide for several Mums
with how's-your-father hampers handy   Eyes
on the ball boys   She's safe in her enclave
that pretty plinth   where all the boundaries end.

College Green

SW1P 3SE

They'd lost the will   or decamped   whichever
feels more like the strapline that pegs tonight's
pause in the triple-speak epic   Friday's
afoot   and plane leaves are left here to flap
in a huff of breeze   Leaving   they've pitched some-
where   right off the kilter of where we once
thought this old storm might be gusting   Five tents
pretend that this studio   London-lawn
England   the self-indicted   nippy side-
show will waft back to where it was   come spring.

Thanks to the editors of these journals, where variations on these poems have appeared: *Envoi, The High Window, A New Ulster, Orbis, The Poetry Village, Pulsar, Runcible Spoon* and *Smoke*.

Part One is one of two. This is a second impression.

Dover Marine Station served boat trains until its closure in 1994.
Fugloy is in the remote north eastern corner of the Faroe Islands.
Bemerton Heath is in west Salisbury, and includes the only non-selective high school in the city.
Alexandra Park is a large business complex in St. Helens, once the headquarters of Pilkington's Glass.
West Bexington was one of the locations used in the third TV series of Broadchurch.
The Deaf Institute and **the Bury Met** are small music venues.
The apartment block in **Torremolinos** was photographed in 1973. Franco died in 1975.
The Land Settlement, Abington recycles with permission titles from Epic45's *Through Broken Summer*, w&w045.
Most of **Vincent Square** is occupied by Westminster School's private playing fields.

Words and pictures are © Will Daunt 2020
ISBN: 9780244580346
£5

Appearing elsewhere:

Lancashire Working
Running Out Of England
The Good Is Abroad
Distant Close
Powerless
Landed
Town Fliers/ Town Criers
Thousands Bourn
Every Dark Advance

Gerard Manley Hopkins: the Lydiate Connections

Edited elsewhere:

Tim Noble: *Writing On Rock*
Eddie Wainwright: *Pleading At The Bar Of Truth*
P.E. Daunt: *Ten Letters To A Grandson*